Visiting a ROMAN CATHOLIC CHURCH

T0125311

Visiting a ROMAN CATHOLIC CHURCH

Danny Sullivan

Photography
KEN DOVER

Illustration/Design
JUDY BILLSON

LUTTERWORTH PRESS
CAMBRIDGE

Lutterworth Press
P.O. Box 60
Cambridge CB1 2NT

British Library Cataloguing in Publication Data available

Copyright © Danny Sullivan 1981

First published in UK 1981 by Lutterworth Press
Reprinted 1988

The author would like to thank the people who offered him advice and criticism during the preparation of the manuscript. He would particularly like to thank Father John, Father Digby and the people of Our lady of Muswell for the warm welcome and encouragement he received from them.

When you look up the passages from the Bible remember that the first number after the name of the book is the chapter number, and the other numbers refer to the verses; so, Mark 15:22–37 is Mark's Gospel, chapter 15, verses 22 to 37. If the verse numbers are written 22, 37 it means verses 22 and 37.

ISBN 0-7188-2470-9

All rights reserved. No part of this publication may be reproduced, stored in a retrieval system, or transmitted in any form or by any means, electronic, mechanical, photocopying, recording, or otherwise, without the prior permission in writing of the publisher.

Printed in Great Britain by
St Edmundsbury Press Limited, Bury St Edmunds, Suffolk

Contents

1. Visiting a Catholic Church 3

2. The Church of Our Lady of Muswell . . . 5

3. The Priests and their work 17

4. Services of worship 29

5. How Our Lady of Muswell is organised . .43

6. The Church as a community 45

7. Over to you 53

    Book list 56

    Index 57

1. Visiting a Catholic Church

The word church means different things to different people. For some, church means a building which they usually see being used on a Sunday. For others, church means much more than simply a building. To these people, church has to do with their way of life. Certainly they may come together on a Sunday to take part in a service, but being a member of the church may mean taking part in other activities too.

You may have looked at a church and wondered what happens when people go inside it. Or you may belong to a church and know something already of what takes place when people come together there.

This book is about a Catholic Church named Our Lady of Muswell. Muswell Hill is in North London. 'Our Lady' refers to Mary who was the mother of Jesus. Muswell Hill is a busy part of North London. There are many houses and shops there. Our Lady of Muswell serves about two thousand Catholics. They are people of all ages – from the very young to the very old.

THE ROMAN CATHOLIC CHURCH

Catholics are part of the Christian Church. They are often called Roman Catholics. So, a Catholic church can be referred to as a Roman Catholic church. This has to do with the history of the Catholic Church. St. Peter, one of the first followers of Jesus and later a leader of the first Christians, is buried in Rome. The Pope, the leader of the Church, lives in Rome and it is there that we find the headquarters of the Church.

The Catholic Church in Britain traces its history back to when St. Augustine first brought Christianity to our shores in the 6th century. Today you will find a Catholic church in every city and town. The history of the Catholic Church in Britain has not always been a peaceful one. You may find it worthwhile and interesting to look this up in a history book or encyclopedia.

In this book you will find out about the Church and people of Our Lady of Muswell. Finding out about this Church and its people may help you to understand about the Catholic Church.

3

Not every Catholic church will be exactly the same though there will be similarities – particularly in services. If there is a Catholic church near you you might like to find out about it and compare it with Our Lady of Muswell.

2.The Church of Our Lady of Muswell

THE HISTORY

The earliest record of a Church with the name of Our Lady of Muswell is the year 1155. That was when a group of **nuns** had a chapel which was dedicated to Our Lady of Muswell. (Nuns are women who have dedicated their lives to God and live together in a convent.) Beside this chapel was a well and many people believed its water had healing powers. They would travel from long distances as pilgrims to come and visit it.

In the time of Henry VIII the English Church broke away from the Roman Catholic Church. The English Church no longer accepted the Pope in Rome as their leader. What happened in Britain during that time is worth finding out about and some reference books are suggested at the end of the book.

One of the things which happened was that Catholic churches were taken over by the English Church or were no longer used. It was a very long time before large Catholic churches were again

A nun who regularly joins in the worship at Our Lady of Muswell.

built and used in this country.

It is not surprising then to discover that for a long period after the time of Henry VIII there were no large Catholic churches in England. When Catholic churches were built again the Catholics from Muswell Hill would travel to the nearest one.

At the beginning of the 20th century the French Government felt the Catholic Church had too much influence in France. This Government was not keen on groups of priests or nuns working in schools. During this time many priests and nuns fled from France. A group of nuns arrived in Muswell Hill. They soon opened a school for Catholic children.

When the school was running to their satisfaction they turned their thoughts to helping to provide a church for the Catholics of Muswell Hill. At first temporary buildings were used as a church while the people tried to raise enough money for the building of a permanent one. The building of the present church was completed in 1938. The Catholics of Muswell Hill were very happy to have their own church again.

THE CHURCH BUILDING

The Church is situated on a very busy road. There is a small driveway leading up to it. There is a brightly painted notice board to the left of the main doors. This informs people of the times of services held in the Church.

Above the main doors, sculpted into the wall, is a figure of Mary holding the child Jesus. Further above this is a large circular window with a cross taking up the central position. At the very top of the Church is a large stone Celtic cross.

Entering the main doors you come to the porch. Here people stop and chat before or after a service. Many notices are on display in the porch. For example, there is a large one for C.A.F.O.D. (Catholic Aid for Overseas Development), a Catholic charity which provides aid to underdeveloped countries. Another notice asks that members of the church pray for all the people who live in a certain road. Each week the name of a different road or street will go up on this notice.

On a table in the porch church newspapers and magazines are for sale. There are rows of hymn books and books which are used during services.

To the left of the porch a door and staircase lead to the choir

The words 'Our Lady' refer to Mary, the mother of Jesus.

You can see the cross at the top of the church from quite a distance.

In the porch people stop to chat and to read the notices.

section. From this position you have a splendid view of the Church as a whole. Here there is the organ and from here the **choir** sometimes sings. Usually the choir joins the other church members downstairs.

When you enter the main part of the Church on your own you are immediately struck by the quiet atmosphere. If other people are present they are usually sitting quietly on their own.

The main passageway down the centre of the Church is known as the **aisle**. On either side of the aisle there are rows of benches. There are many things on the walls and round the Church to catch your eye. There are small rooms at the back which are used for the sacrament of **confession** (see chapter 4).

At the very front is the **sanctuary**. Sanctuary means holy place. It is from here that the priest will lead the members of the church in the service. There is a large **altar** at the back of the sanctuary. An altar is like a long table. Over this altar there is a large canopy. On the altar there are six large candles. For many Christians the candle is a symbol of light and goodness. Candles, when lit, give a warm and reassuring glow.

A small room at the back of the church is used for confession.

The sanctuary and altar are at the front of the church.

On this altar there is also a **tabernacle**. The tabernacle is like a safe and has a door which can be locked. In it are kept **hosts** (round pieces of wafer) which are blessed during the service known as Eucharist. Usually Catholics call this service Mass.

To the right of the altar is a door which leads to the **vestry**. This is where the priest puts on the special clothes – known as vestments – which he uses for the different services. Near to the entrance to the vestry and attached to the wall is a large lamp known as the **sanctuary lamp**. The lamp is always lit and serves as a reminder that you are in a holy place.

Further down in front of the large altar is a smaller altar. This one faces out towards the members of the church and is the one most often used for services. To the left of this altar there is a **lectern**. This is where the priest and members of the church read during the service. The readings are always taken from some part of the Bible.

Just in front of this altar there are marble **altar rails** which separate the whole of the sanctuary from the rest of the Church. Most modern Catholic churches will not have these rails. This is because many changes took place in Catholic churches from

The hosts are blessed during the Mass and kept in the tabernacle.

The sanctuary lamp burns all the time.

The Bible readings are contained in a lectionary on the lectern.

1963 – after a great Council which was held in Rome. This was called the Second Vatican Council. Catholic bishops from all over the world met in Rome for many months. They discussed important aspects of what Catholics believe and how the Church is governed.

This Church also has two **side altars** – so called because they are to the sides of the main sanctuary area. Around each of these altars is an inscription in Latin. This is what is written,

Jesu Dulcis Corde Miserere Nobis.
Ave Maria Immaculata In Coelum Gloriose Assumpta.

In English these would mean:-

Gentle heart of Jesus, have mercy on us.
Hail, Immaculate Mary, who was gloriously raised into heaven.

For hundreds of years Latin was the language used in church services. It was the language of those who could read and write. So when churches were built inscriptions and quotations from the Bible would be in Latin. It was only after the Second Vatican Council that Catholic churches in Britain began to use English in

The side altars are often used for private prayer and people kneel and meditate there.

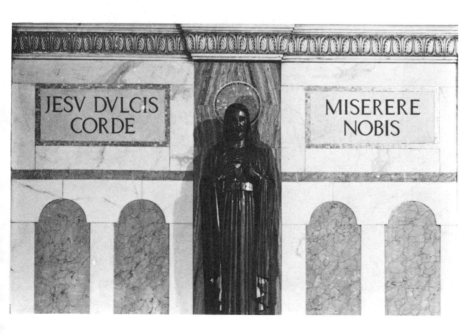

their services. Before that Latin was used and church members could follow the English translation in a book called a **missal**.

In front of both these altars you will find a large stand which holds many candles. We have mentioned earlier the symbolism of the candle. Members of the church will often come and light a candle – stopping to pray silently about some good they may have experienced or to pray that good will come to those close to them.

Catholic churches often have **statues** in them. These may be of Jesus, Mary or a saint. A saint is a person who led a life that the Church feels is an example to all its members. Countries have patron saints.

There is also a **pulpit** and beside it a large cross with the figure of Jesus on it. This is called a crucifix. In days past the priest would have preached a sermon from here. When English began to be used in services in Catholic churches in 1963 other changes took place as well. One of these was that the pulpit was used less and less for preaching the sermon. In some churches it may still be used but on the whole the priest will preach his sermon from the altar area.

People light candles as symbols of light and goodness.

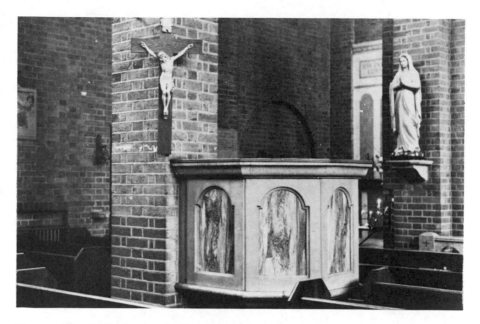

The crucifix reminds people that Jesus died on a cross.

Around the two main walls are fourteen sculptures – seven on each wall. These are known as the **Stations of the Cross**. These sculptures depict the hours of Jesus' life from when he was arrested until he died. They show what happened to him and the route he had to take when carrying his cross (see Mark 15:1–47). Today Christians still visit Jerusalem and follow the route depicted in these sculptures.

During the period of the Church's year known as Lent (leading up to Easter), members of the church take part in a service following the sculptures from beginning to end. Prayers are said and thoughts are shared about what happened to Jesus during the last days of his life. The history of these sculptures goes back to the time when most people could not read or write. Sculptures such as the Stations of the Cross explained parts of the Christian message to these people.

The windows of this Church are very high up. They are not specially coloured or decorated. However, the windows of many churches, especially old ones, are particularly attractive and decorative. They are coloured in such a way as to reflect light very beautifully. This adds to the atmosphere of a church.

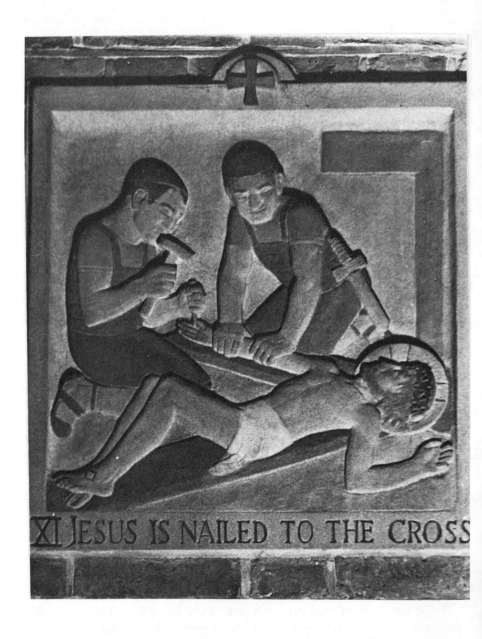

XI JESUS IS NAILED TO THE CROSS

Fourteen sculptures on the walls show what happened to Jesus during the days leading to his death. They are known as the Stations of the Cross and this is number eleven.

3. The Priests and their work

When Jesus was alive his followers were known as disciples (see Luke 6:12–16). Jesus stressed to his disciples the importance of being a servant to others. He was not afraid to be of service to the disciples himself even though he was their leader (see John 13:1–16).

Members of the Catholic Church see connections between their priests and the disciples; men ready to serve their community and also men to whom people will look for guidance and help.

At the time of writing there are three priests at Our Lady of Muswell. Father John, who is in charge of the Church, is known as the parish priest; Father Digby, his assistant, is known as a curate or an assistant priest. The third priest is Father Joe. He is doing some study at a college in London and then he hopes to go to a country overseas and work as a priest there. Father Joe helps Father John and Father Digby when he can – especially

with the Sunday services. Priests are called Father because they are seen as the head of the parish 'family'.

TRAINING TO BE A PRIEST

Training to be a priest takes a long time – at least six years. This is because there is much to learn! As a leader of the church community the priest leads all the services. He will learn why services are taken and what are the history and traditions behind them. He will learn much about the history of the Catholic Church, why it has its rules and why it holds the views it does on many matters.

Father John and Father Digby spend much time helping people in their community. Their training will try to help them prepare for this. When they were student priests they may have worked during their holidays in a hospital or with children who are in care.

Some student priests have spent time helping priests who are already working in churches. This gives them an idea of what they themselves will have to do as priests.

The priest regularly visits elderly people in a home.

Children at the local school look forward to Father John's visits.

When Father John and Father Digby completed their training they became priests in a special service known as **ordination** (see chapter 4). This service was led by the Bishop of the area. The Bishop is in charge of all the churches in his area, and more will be said about him later.

THE WORK OF A PRIEST

Father John and Father Digby lead busy lives. They are involved in some kind of church service every day of the week. They also visit members of their Church in their homes. Sometimes they may hold a service there. This helps them come to know a particular family and their friends better.

One day during the week either Father John or Father Digby visits the sick of the parish and shares a short service with them. They may also receive a telephone call in the middle of the night telling them that one of the members of the church is very ill and wants his priest to be with him, in which case they will go.

Father John and Father Digby sometimes visit an old people's home, a hospital, a home for handicapped children, and a prison. They also visit the local Catholic schools. This happens more frequently, perhaps, with their local Junior School. The timetable of the Junior School makes it easier to visit. A class from the school will prepare a service and Father Digby will come and share it with them.

At Our Lady of Muswell some of the children came from the Junior School to visit Father Digby in the Church. They were there for the Mass, a service at which adults were present. When the service had ended Father Digby told the children to feel free to look around. It wasn't long before there was a great hub of noise as investigations got under way. This was in contrast to the quiet atmosphere you usually find in churches! Many interesting questions were asked about some of the objects which have already been described in this book. Father Digby had prepared well for this visit and was ready for the questions!

After the children had looked round the Church Father Digby treated them to lemonade and biscuits and then answered some personal questions. Questions such as,

Do you want to be a priest for ever? Yes, was Father Digby's answer, explaining he had only decided to become a priest after a very great deal of thought and prayer.

Why can't girls be priests? Father Digby said that this was a law of the Church. However, Church laws can be changed and perhaps in the future it might be possible for girls to become priests.

Would you like to be a Bishop? A very definite no was Father Digby's answer to this! He felt a Bishop's life was very different from that of a priest. The Bishop had to spend a great deal of time visiting the many churches in his Diocese. He also had meetings and conferences to attend. Father Digby felt that this made it harder for a Bishop to get close to people.

Have you ever felt like a big sneeze during service? No, but he did feel once that he was going to have an attack of the hiccups. Luckily he didn't!

We have described the work of Father John and Father Digby in quite a bit of detail. Yet they would be the first to say that every member of the church is as valuable to God as they are. They would say that all the members of the church are trying to live thoughtful, Christian lives – though that is not always easy. Also members of the church should not only care about each other but about all people – especially those in need (see Matthew 25:34–40).

A PRIEST'S SPECIAL CLOTHES

We all wear special clothes for special occasions. So it is with Father John and Father Digby. When they are taking services they wear special clothes called **vestments**. They are linked to the history and tradition of the Church – especially to the time of Jesus and those first Christians who followed his teachings after his death.

During the day a Catholic priest wears a black or grey suit and what has become known as the 'dog collar'. This is a round, white collar though a more modern version only shows a small part of it at the front. The history of the dog collar goes back to the early 19th century. Clergymen wore a simple, plain white neckerchief which eventually changed to a white collar fastened at the back. It was usually worn with black. When they are relaxing and having a day off they may wear casual clothes as we do.

The following special clothes are worn during the Eucharist or Mass.

Amice A square or oblong piece of linen to which two long

The amice is tied on with two long tapes.

The alb is sometimes embroidered or it can be plain.

The priest ties the cincture round his waist to keep the alb in place.

tapes are attached at the upper corners. The priest would place this over his shoulder and tie it round his waist. In Roman times the amice was a hood which was dropped over one's shoulders when indoors.

Alb A long white linen robe which is gathered round the waist. The alb was originally an undergarment worn by the Romans.

Cincture A long cord which the priest wears round his waist to keep the alb in place. In Roman times it was worn to keep the alb secure so that the wearer could walk or work freely.

Stole A narrow piece of material worn round the neck. This seems to have developed from having been part of a larger scarf or shawl.

Chasuble A large outer garment. A chasuble can be richly embroidered or of a very simple design. In Roman times it was a heavy outer garment used when travelling. It had an opening for the head and completely covered the person wearing it. In Latin it was called **Casula** which means 'little house'.

For other services the priest only wears some of these special clothes. At times he wears a **cassock** which is like a long black coat. Over this he may wear a **surplice** which is a white linen garment.

The special clothes can vary in colour. Each colour symbolises something special. The Church uses these colours to help remind its members of the different ways they can understand their Christian lives.

White is the symbol of joy. This is used when celebrating the feast days of saints and is also used now in services for the dead.

Red is the symbol of love. This helps remind the church members that God loves them and that they should love and care for one another.

Green is the symbol of hope. This colour is used on days which are not special feast days.

Purple is the symbol of repentance. An important part of a Christian's life is being able to be sorry.

Black is the symbol of death and mourning. This is used at funerals or at services remembering the dead. White is now used for these services also. This is to show that Christians believe there is a life after death.

The stole is also kept in place by the cincture.

The chasuble is often richly embroidered, like this one.

4. Services of worship

People sometimes celebrate special events in life – like birth and marriage. They mourn when someone close to them dies. They would be concerned if a member of their family were ill. They would want them to recover. In the Catholic Church there are special services known as the **sacraments**. These are related to events which happen in our lives.

In the Catholic Church there are seven special services which have this name. These sacraments are meant to be symbols of life for Catholics. Each one has its own special meaning and is linked to the history of the Church. We will look at these sacraments one by one and find out how and when they take place at Our Lady of Muswell.

BAPTISM

Baptism takes place when a person is welcomed as a new mem-

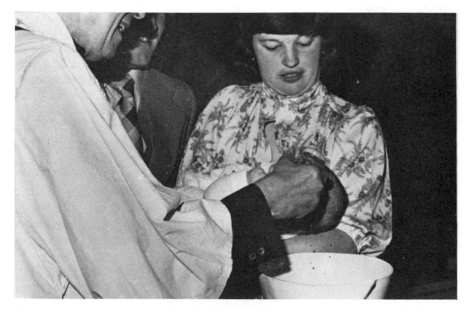

At a baptism water is poured over the baby's head.

ber of the Church. This person can be a newly born baby, young child or adult. The baptism may take place on its own or during the service known as the Mass.

Water is used during baptism. It is put into a special container called a **font**. Father John pours a very small amount over the head of the person being baptised. Water has always been a symbol of new life. In baptism it is used to symbolise that the person being baptised is becoming a new member of the Christian Church. While pouring the water the priest will say,

I baptise you in the name of the Father and of the Son and of the Holy Spirit.

The person's family and friends are present at the baptism. They and all the church members present welcome him as a member of the Church through baptism. They promise to care for him.

Baptism also recalls the fact that Jesus was baptised by John the Baptist in the river Jordan (see Mark 1:9–11).

When a baby is baptised the word Christening is sometimes used. This is because the child is being given a Christian name.

CONFIRMATION

Confirmation is linked very closely to baptism. Christians believe that God's Holy Spirit can give them strength at Confirmation to lead caring, thoughtful lives. A Christian is only confirmed once.

At Our Lady of Muswell confirmation takes place every couple of years. The Bishop takes the service and he is assisted by Father John and Father Digby.

In England children are usually confirmed at thirteen or fourteen. Of course, adults may be confirmed at the service too. Being confirmed gives Christians the task of committing themselves to the kind of life Jesus asked of his followers.

Confirmation usually takes place during the Mass. The Bishop lays his hands on each person who comes up to him. The history of this can be found in the Bible (Acts 8:17). He puts **chrism**, a kind of oil, on their foreheads. This symbolises each person as a full member of God's own people and is another reference to the first Christians (see 1 Peter 2:9).

The Bishop will also give each person a light slap on the cheek. This is a medieval custom which means that the person may not find life as a Christian easy. There may be people against him

Father John may explain part of the gospel reading in his sermon.

because he is a Christian. After this the Bishop says to the person, 'Peace be with you.'

THE EUCHARIST

The word Eucharist means thanksgiving. The Eucharist has a long tradition and history behind it, and is referred to by Catholics as the Mass.

Jesus was a Jew. When he ate his last meal with his followers before his death, known as the Last Supper, that meal was Jewish. At that meal Jesus shared bread and wine with his followers and said some words (see 1 Cor. 11:25). He also said to them, 'As often as you do this, you shall do it in memory of me.'

After his death Jesus' followers used to meet every Sunday to celebrate the Eucharist and to remember him. This is what the Catholics of Muswell Hill are doing when they come to Mass on a Sunday or on any other day of the week.

If you read about Jesus' last meal with his followers you will see that it was a very simple affair. Often when Father John or Father Digby go to a church member's house and celebrate the

Children take the offertory from the back of the church up to the altar.

Father John prays at the altar during the Mass.

Eucharist with them and their family and friends, it will seem very simple and homely.

In the church, especially on a Sunday, it is much more organised because so many members attend. There are readings from the Bible, usually read by members of the church. The first reading is normally from the Old Testament and the second from the New Testament. Both readings may be about the same idea. In between these readings the people in church recite a psalm from the Old Testament.

Father John will then read from one of the gospels in the New Testament. After this he shares some of his thoughts with the people, in which he may explain parts of the readings or suggest how he and all those present can try to live better lives as Christians. This part of the service is called the **sermon**.

After the sermon all say the **creed** together. In this prayer they express their belief in God, in Jesus and in the life of the Church.

Following the creed we come to the part of the service known as the **offertory**. This is when people take offerings to the altar. First of all, prayers are said. Usually these prayers are for the people present but they also remember those in need – the poor,

Father John blesses the hosts before giving them to the congregation.

Father John returns to the altar after distributing the hosts.

the hungry. If there is a war going on somewhere or if a disaster has occurred somewhere prayers will be said for those involved. A hymn is sung. A small procession takes place from the back of the Church to the altar. Families take it in turn to have responsibility for this. They will bring up the jars and cup which are used during the rest of the service. Money, which has been collected during the singing of the hymn, will also be presented. These gifts are received by Father John and the boy who is assisting him at the altar. The priest and the people pray together, offering these gifts and their lives to God.

These prayers lead up to the part of the Eucharist which remembers the Last Supper. This is known as the **consecration**. All is silent except for Father John who continues to pray out loud. He blesses the hosts to be used at communion time. As this is a very important part of the Eucharist a bell is solemnly rung twice.

After the consecration prayers are said for all those present and their families and friends. All remember, too, their relatives and friends who have died. All say the Lord's Prayer, the Our Father, (see Matthew 6:7–15) and then comes the time when the people shake hands with one another. This is known as the handshake of peace. It reminds the church members that they all belong to the same community and that they should care for one another.

The church members then go up to the altar rails and receive a host (see chapter 2) from Father John. They may receive this host in their mouth or in their hands before placing it in their mouths themselves. This part of the service is known as Holy Communion. Adults and children from the age of seven upwards may take part in it, provided that they have been baptised in the Catholic Church.

After this there is a time of silence and then more prayers. The service ends with Father John blessing the church members. Before they leave he reminds them of services and events which are to take place during the week.

At different times during this service there may be hymn singing. The hymns may be accompanied by organ playing or there may be more modern hymns with guitar accompaniment. At Our Lady of Muswell you will find that the church members don't let the choir do all the singing!

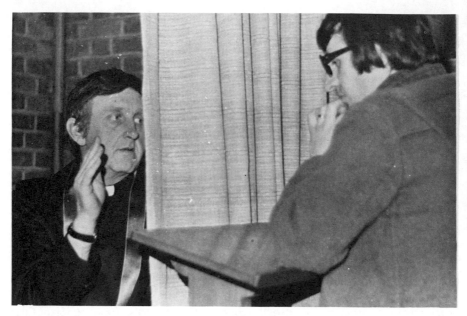

A man asks for God's forgiveness at confession.

CONFESSION

Father John and Father Digby share this sacrament with their church members at the times displayed on the church notice-board. They may use the rooms that were mentioned earlier.

Confession for Catholics is the sign of the forgiveness of God. If they have done wrong in their lives then through confession they ask God's forgiveness. They tell the priest how they feel they have done wrong. The priest prays with them, offers them advice as to how they can live a better Christian life and then assures them that their wrongs are forgiven in the name of Jesus. Father John and Father Digby make their confession too – to another priest. They do not think they are perfect!

Father John or Father Digby may also suggest to church members that they say some special prayers because of their wrong doing. They may suggest that they do something difficult, like being thoughtful and helpful to someone they don't like. These suggestions are to help the person to think about the wrongs they have done and to encourage them in their willingness to live a better Christian life.

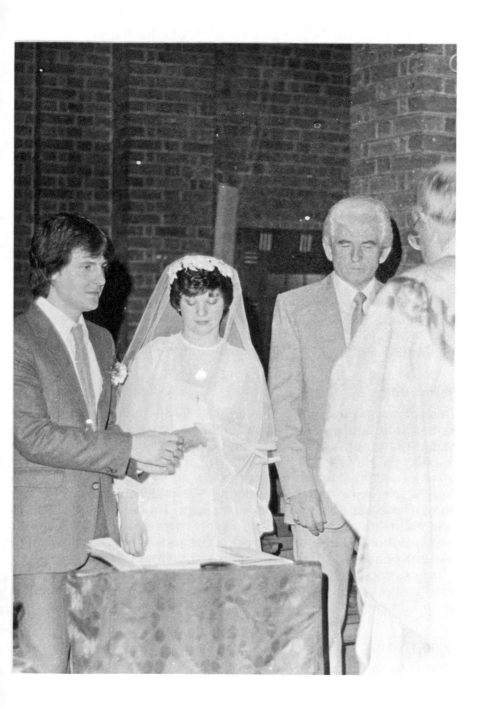

Nowadays people do not need to go into a special room for confession. If they wish they may talk with a priest face to face. There are also other times when the church members together remember in silence, the wrongs they have done and ask God's forgiveness.

Confession is not easy, but Catholics (like other Christians) feel it is important to understand what forgiveness is about and also to have the courage to admit doing wrong.

MARRIAGE

At Our Lady of Muswell the service of marriage usually takes place during a Mass. As church members the two people to be married are present with their family and friends. By making promises to God they show that they take marriage very seriously. They ask God's help because they know that life together will not always be easy – it will be full of ups and downs.

Weddings at Our Lady of Muswell usually take place on a Saturday but they can take place any day. Special Bible readings and hymns are chosen to fit in with the theme of marriage.

ORDINATION

This sacrament used to be called Holy Orders. This is the service Father John and Father Digby took part in when they had completed their training and became priests. This service is taken by the Bishop. He lays his hands on the student priest as do all the priests present. The student priest is reminded during this service of the work he is undertaking. He is asked to care for the people to whose church he will be sent. He will be expected to lead them in worship and be involved in the kinds of things Father John and Father Digby do. The family and friends of the student priest are there with him on this important occasion.

This service would only take place at Our Lady of Muswell if a student priest came from that church. Usually the service takes place in a cathedral.

ANOINTING OF THE SICK

Reference to this sacrament is made in the New Testament (see James 5: 14–16).

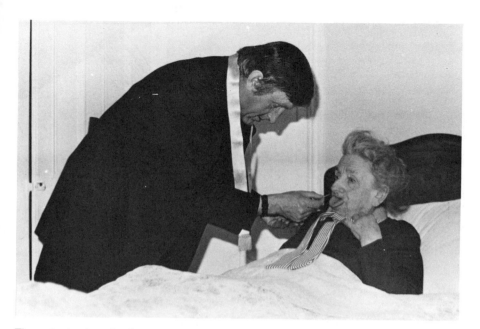

The priest takes the hosts to people who are too ill to go to church.

Illness can be a difficult and trying time. This sacrament is used to let church members know that though they are too ill to come to church they are not forgotten. Father John will visit the home of the sick person to take this service.

The family of the sick person are present. Father John prays with the family and then he anoints the sick person. The sick person receives a host from Father John just as he or she would if they were well enough to attend Mass in church.

If someone is very ill and in hospital then Father John or Father Digby visits the person there.

SPECIAL DAYS

Like other churches Our Lady of Muswell holds special services at certain times of the year.

At **Christmas** time a Mass is held at midnight. Carols are sung before and during the service, recalling the birth of Jesus (see Luke 2:1–20).

During the week leading up to Easter Sunday there are special services on Palm Sunday, Maundy Thursday and Good Friday.

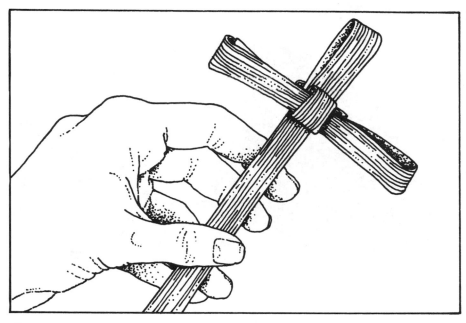

Palm crosses are given to remind people that Jesus died on a cross.

Palm Sunday recalls when Jesus was greeted very enthusiastically by the people of Jerusalem (see John 12: 12–14). They waved palm leaves and placed them on Jesus' route. This was to show their respect for him. At Palm Sunday Mass Father John will bless palms and the church members will take them away as a reminder of that day.

Maundy Thursday recalls the evening when Jesus shared the Last Supper with his close followers. It is the one which is remembered in the Eucharist.

Good Friday recalls the day Jesus was put to death on a cross (see Luke 23:26–34). On this day the church looks very bare. There are no flowers, and crosses and statues are covered with purple cloths.

Easter celebrates the Christian belief that Jesus was seen by his followers after his death (see Luke 24:36–43). It is a time of special joy. Easter Sunday explains why Sunday is a special day for the Church. The church is very brighly decorated with flowers and the covers are removed from the crosses and statues. This makes a great contrast to the bare looking church of Good Friday.

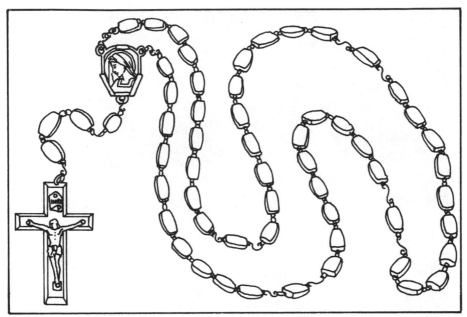

Many people use Rosary beads to help them when they pray. Each bead represents a prayer to be said.

On special feast days there may be a procession at Our Lady of Muswell. This involves walking round the Church and singing hymns. Prayers will be said also.

Another important day, is when children receive the host for the first time. This is called their **First Holy Communion**. All their families attend and it is a day of happiness for all the members of the church. Children are usually prepared for this day with the help of their teachers at school and their parents at home.

At Our Lady of Muswell a service is sometimes held known as **Benediction**. This consists mainly of prayers and hymns which are sung in the evening. Sometimes there may be a reading from the Bible. A prayer known as the **Rosary** may be said during Benediction. Beads are used when praying the Rosary. Each bead represents a prayer to be said. The main prayer used is one known as the 'Hail Mary' – a prayer in honour of Mary, Jesus' mother.

Wicker baskets are handed round for the collection.

5. How Our Lady of Muswell is organised

We have mentioned before that Our Lady of Muswell is some-times visited by its Bishop. This Bishop, the Archbishop of West-minster, has responsibility for the **Diocese of Westminster**.

Bishops in the Church are first referred to in its early history – about the year 100 AD when a Christian writer by the name of Ignatius tells Christians to be obedient to their Bishops.

In the same way today, Catholics look on their Bishops as leaders. As the Bishop cannot visit all his churches regularly, because of the demands on his time, he will often write them **Pastoral letters**. These letters will be about how he and all the members of the churches can best try to live their lives as Christ-ians. He will visit churches when it is time for the sacrament of confirmation.

All the people in his diocese are under the Bishop's authority. It is he who decided which priests would be in charge of the Church of Our Lady of Muswell. Father John and Father Digby have the responsibility of involving all the members in the life of the Church.

Father John and Father Digby live in a house which adjoins the Church and is known as the **presbytery**. The cost of running the house needs to be met, as does the cost of lighting and heating the Church. Money comes from the church members. They provide it by placing it in an offering plate or by making a **covenant**. With a covenant, a member promises to pay the church a certain amount of money every year. The church can also claim back the tax paid on that money.

At Sunday service there are usually two money collections. The first is for the general needs of the Church of Our Lady of Muswell and the Diocese. The second is usually for something special, for example to help train priests, to help Catholic church-es overseas who are in need or to help with the cost of building a local Catholic school.

Father John and Father Digby are allowed by their Bishop to have a small amount of money for their own personal needs. They also use some of the Church's money to run their cars. At Easter and Christmas time there is a special collection for the

The summer fete raises money to meet the church's different needs.

priests. The money collected is given by the church members for Father John and Father Digby's personal use. The people of Our Lady of Muswell are very generous indeed to their priests.

Recently the Catholic Church has been trying to involve church members more in the whole life of the church. To do this churches have appointed **parish councils**. These councils will help with all sorts of matters, from suggestions about worship to ideas about raising money. The council meetings are an opportunity for church members to air their views about church life. Not every Catholic church has a parish council. Our Lady of Muswell does not have one at the moment. However, there are plenty of members of the church who will do readings during the service, help organise meetings and plan the church's summer fete.

6. The Church as a community

We have looked at the services of worship at Our Lady of Muswell. We have seen that Father John and Father Digby lead busy lives.

To be a Christian means more than attending services of worship. It means having and showing thought and care for others because you believe in Jesus' message. Different members of the church come together – sometimes to take part in a group activity to be of help to others.

This chapter describes some of the groups which come together at Our Lady of Muswell. Not everyone in the church will belong to a group. Some may not have the time to, others may not wish to. They may live their Christian lives by trying to be good parents or by trying to be a good example at work – through being thoughtful and caring.

THE JUSTICE AND PEACE GROUP

The members are particularly concerned about justice and peace throughout the world. As Christians they believe that every person has basic human rights. They are aware that in many countries of the world people are not allowed these rights. The members meet once a month and sometimes involve members of the other Christian churches in the area. They meet in a member's house and there may be up to thirty people present. Some of the time is spent praying and thinking. Then time is given over to discussing group activities. At the end of the meeting the members will pause to think and pray again.

The group has helped to raise money for the victims of violence in Northern Ireland. It is in touch with members of different Christian churches in Belfast. It has sent money to these members in Belfast and they have used it to help boys and girls – both Protestant and Catholic – to go on holiday together to Nottingham.

The members have also taken part in an all night vigil. Taking part in a vigil means giving witness to something you believe in. The vigil was for human rights. During the night they listened to

all kinds of readings about human rights. They prayed together and at other times they prayed quietly on their own. They linked the vigil with the **United Nations Day** for International Peace and Justice. They also knew that at this time of the year (end of October) Christians in other churches were holding vigils or having specific events related to human rights.

CATHOLIC AID FOR OVERSEAS DEVELOPMENT

The people of Our Lady of Muswell who belong to the **C.A.F.O.D.** group (Catholic Aid for Overseas Development) raise money on behalf of countries where there are serious shortages of food, medical aid, schools and such things as machinery for farming the land.

As well as raising money the members sometimes put on a display of photographs and information at the back of the Church explaining the work of C.A.F.O.D.

Jesus told his followers always to remember those people who are in great need (see Matthew 25:34–40). The members of C.A.F.O.D. feel that they are trying to do this. Besides raising

The Discussion Group talks about a reading from the Bible.

money all the year round and providing information about C.A.F.O.D., they make a special effort (twice a year). They ask all the other church members to join them. They ask that the adults in a family go without one of their daily meals – either lunch, tea or dinner – and give the money they would have spent on it to C.A.F.O.D. Many of the church members join with the C.A.F.O.D. group in doing this.

The **Bible Discussion Group** meets to study passages from the Bible in more detail. They discuss these selected passages, sharing their own thoughts and ideas about them. In particular they study the teachings of Jesus and the life of the first Christians.

The **Legion of Mary** takes its name in honour of Mary, Jesus' mother. The members of this group try to be aware of people in their area who are in need. They like to help people in a practical way. Thus, if someone is ill and alone one of the group may visit the person regularly and also do their shopping. The group want to do this without embarrassing people. They do not expect the people they help to join their church. They help because, for them, it is an important part of being a Christian.

The **Wednesday Afternoon Group** is organised by some ladies of the Church. They open the church hall and prepare tea and biscuits for any pensioners who live nearby. When the pensioners arrive they have the opportunity to sit and chat or play bingo as well as have their tea and biscuits. For some of the pensioners this afternoon might be the only opportunity they have of sitting and chatting with other people.

The young people who belong to the **Scouts, Cubs and Brownies** meet in the church hall. The adults responsible for them are members of the Church. Like other groups of their age, there are times when they meet with scouts, cubs and brownies from all over the country.

A group of young people who are keen to learn **Irish dancing** also meet in the church hall. There they are taught by an adult. They have the opportunity of entering graded competitions and receive medals and shields which record their progress. When the Church or school holds a fete they may perform at that.

These are not the only groups in the church of Our Lady of Muswell. Sometimes many of the church members will come together for a special occasion. This could be for a church dance, a folk-song evening, church fete or a presentation evening if one

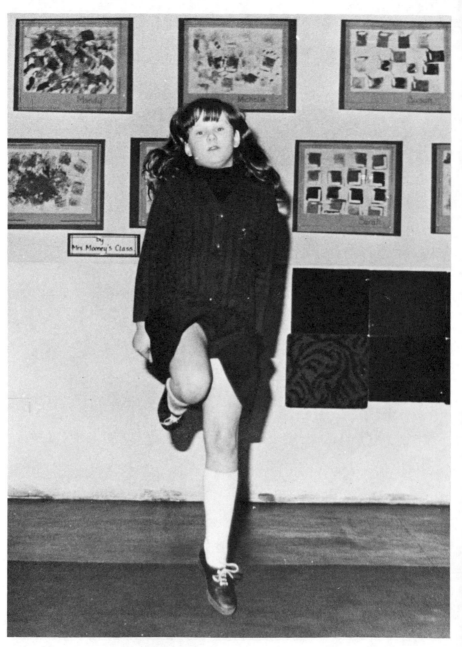

The Irish dance group enjoys entering competitions.

of the priests were leaving to go to another church.

While Our Lady of Muswell might seem to do well for groups it would not be fair to say that all members of the Church belong to one. People decide this for themselves.

Over to you!

7. Over to you

This book has told you something about the life of the people who attend the Church of Our Lady of Muswell. It is not a famous church! The people who belong to it come from all walks of life. Some may be more involved in the life of the Church than others. Most church members come together on a Sunday. It is up to each one to decide how to try to live as a Christian the rest of the week.

The people belonging to the Church are friendly. If you were a visitor you would be made to feel welcome.

Perhaps you can find out about a Catholic church near you. Keeping in mind the chapters of this book you might like to compare it with Our Lady of Muswell. A good way of doing this would be to receive permission to visit the church. As well as seeing round the church perhaps one of the priests would show you the vestments which are worn during services.

Children practise hard their singing for the class Mass.

Many Catholic churches have statues on the walls like this one.

It would be helpful if you could visit the church when a service is being held. Find out your own thoughts and reactions to what is happening. What about the people attending the service? They may be willing to talk to you afterwards.

It is worth recording information. You might wish to write down or record in some way what you discover. A cassette recorder is useful when interviewing people. Many parts inside the church will lend themselves to sketching and photography. You could build up an attractive file of your work in this way.

Once you have found out about a Catholic church near you, you may find it interesting to learn about other places of worship. Do they seem very different from a Catholic church? Are their services different? Do the church members become involved in activities like those of Our Lady of Muswell? Do they have some of the things that Our Lady of Muswell has, for example, a Celtic Cross, Latin inscriptions?

In Britain today there are places of worship belonging to people who are Christians, Jews, Sikhs, Hindus, Muslims, and Buddhists. There may be opportunities for you to make many interesting comparisons.

Book List

Church buildings
P. J. Hunt, *Churches and Chapels*, Watts
H. & R. Leacroft, *Churches and Cathedrals*, Lutterworth
P. J. Hunt, *What to look for inside a church*, Ladybird
P. J. Hunt, *What to look for outside a church*, Ladybird
H. Pluckrose, *Churches*, Mills & Boon

I. Calvert, *Churches in Britain*, Basil Blackwell

History
P. Tilney, *Tudors and Stuarts*, chapters 3 and 4, Mills & Boon

In this series
G. Palmer, *Visiting a Community Church*, Lutterworth
S. Tompkins, *Visiting an Anglican Church*, Lutterworth
D. K. Babraa, *Visiting a Sikh Temple*, Lutterworth

Index

aisle, 9
alb, 26
altar, 9
altar rails, 10, 35
amice, 22
anointing of the sick, 38

baptism, 29, 30
Benediction, 41
Bible group, 48
Bishop, 21, 22, 30, 31, 38, 43

C. A. F. O. D., 47
candle, 9, 14
canopy, 9
cassock, 26
Catholic, 3
Celtic cross, 6
chapel, 5
chasuble, 26
choir, 9
Church, 3
cincture, 26
confession, 36, 38
confirmation, 30, 43
consecration, 35
covenant, 43
creed, 33
curate, 17
crucifix, 14

Diocese, 43
disciple, 17
dog collar, 22

Easter, 40
Eucharist, 10, 31, 33, 40

font, 30

gospel, 33
Good Friday, 40

Holy Communion, 35, 41
hosts, 10, 35, 39

Justice and Peace, 45

Last Supper, 31, 40
Latin, 12
lectern, 10
Lent, 15

marriage, 38
Mass, 10, 21, 30, 31, 38, 39, 40
Maundy Thursday, 40
missal, 14

New Testament, 33, 38
nun, 5

offertory, 33
Old Testament, 33
ordination, 21, 38

Palm Sunday, 40
Parish Council, 44
parish priest, 17
pastoral letter, 43
Pope, 3, 5
porch, 6
priest, 6, 9, 10, 14, 21, 22, 26, 36, 38, 43
psalm, 33
pulpit, 14

Roman Catholic Church, 3, 5
rosary, 41

sacraments, 29
saint, 14
sanctuary, 9
sanctuary lamp, 10
sermon, 14, 33
side altars, 12
Stations of the Cross, 15
statues, 14, 40
stole, 26
surplice, 26

tabernacle, 10

vestments, 22
vestry, 10